T0166041

# Communication Tips
## *for*
## Successful
## Donor Visits

# Communication Tips
## *for*
# Successful
# Donor Visits

By
Dale Wallenius

# Communication Tips for Successful Donor Visits

*iUniverse books may be ordered through booksellers or by contacting:*

*iUniverse*
*1663 Liberty Drive*
*Bloomington, IN 47403*
*www.iuniverse.com*
*1-800-Authors (1-800-288-4677)*

*ISBN: 978-1-4401-1551-6 (sc)*

*Print information available on the last page.*

*iUniverse rev. date: 05/23/2019*

# Introduction

Strong communication skills are vital to fundraising professionals, board members and volunteers.

The difference between success and failure when visiting with donors is understanding how to effectively communicate, how to question with purpose, how to listen attentively, how to analyze nonverbal messages and how to concisely present ideas.

Learn how to achieve maximum results using specific communication tips designed to stimulate every step of the donor visit. The ability to communicate skillfully and confidently with donors is the most important personal skill you can possess.

As a young college fundraiser, one of my first visits with a donor was with Geraldine. She was a consecutive year donor to the college and I thought it would be a good idea to talk to her.

We met at her home for over an hour. I told Geraldine all about myself, the college and the capital campaign we were developing. I thoroughly enjoyed myself and thought that the visit went very well.

When I returned to my office, I tried to complete a

Donor Contact Form. It asked about the visit and what I learned about Geraldine's interests, family, education, experiences, likes, dislikes, jobs, community involvement and why she gives money to the college. I could not answer any of the questions. I had not learned anything about Geraldine during our visit.

I went to see Geraldine for a second visit. This time I asked meaningful questions, carefully listened and displayed a genuine, sincere interest and concern for Geraldine. I discovered that this remarkable woman was 87 years old and had no children. I learned that Geraldine was one of our country's first women aviators. Geraldine became very animated when she spoke about her years as an elementary school teacher and how deeply she values education and the college. I listened as Geraldine told me about her parents gifting her stock in blue chip companies many years ago.

Unfortunately, Geraldine died soon after our second visit. A few months after her death, I received a phone call from an attorney telling me that Geraldine had left the college some money in her will.

As the attorney later handed me a check in the amount of $1,196,000, I noted the date on Geraldine's updated will. The date was one week after our second visit.

Fundraising is truly about what you ask and how you listen, not what you say.

Powerful communication skills can propel you to fundraising success and personal achievement.

These communication tips are practical, proven techniques for communicating effectively with all types of donors. You will be able to build stronger and better relationships with donors. Learning vital interpersonal communication skills can reward you for years to come.

Nothing says more about your competence, confidence and professionalism than your human relations skills. Those who are recognized as skilled in communication enjoy the respect of everyone.

Learning and using valuable, insightful communication tips will equip you with practical, proven interpersonal skills and techniques that will make a positive difference when visiting donors.

Bottom line— proven and practical communication tips will enable you to engage *more* donors and *more* potential donors in *more* productive and successful visits.

Learning and using exceptionally powerful interpersonal communication tips and skills will make a positive difference in your career and in your life.

# Table of Contents

# The Donor Visit

The keys to intelligent engagement with a donor—your communication skills, your questions, your listening ability, your positive attitude and your ideas.

*

You can only convince donors of what you believe yourself.

*

Talking is easy. Effective communication with a donor requires skill and practice.

*

\*

You can drive a visit with a donor or let the visit drive you.

\*

Understand the inner workings of the donor visit. Know what you want to accomplish every minute and have your GPS system ready to alter your course.

\*

You must be able to describe the goal of your visit to yourself in one sentence. If not, your fuzzy focus will be confusing to the donor.

\*

\*

Have a clear structure of your visit in your mind. What key points do you want the donor to remember?

\*

When greeting a donor, pay attention to your handshake, eye contact, body language, smile, posture, clothing and tone of voice.

\*

*

Your goal is to connect with donors during visits. Make communication personal and connect with their hearts.

*

\*

Your speaking skills are critical at the beginning of a visit because they create an impression and set a tone for the rest of the visit.

\*

Have and keep disciplined enthusiasm in your voice. Your voice should express sincerity and expertise. How you use your voice is a key to your identity with a donor. It is your personal trademark and serves as a calling card with donors.

\*

\*

Have a 30-second elevator speech ready to use. It demonstrates that you know your organization and can communicate it effectively.

\*

Donors pay attention to folks they believe have something important to say to them.

\*

Be a friend. Donors want to communicate with their friends.

\*

\*

Display a genuine, sincere interest and concern for a donor. You can make a more significant impression on a donor in 10 minutes if you show interest in that person, than if you were to spend one year talking about your organization or yourself.

\*

Your dialogue with a donor must be natural and flexible, yet planned and controlled.

\*

One of your communication objectives with a donor must be achieving a shared understanding.

\*

\*

Think "You"—as in donor. Donors want to hear about themselves—what's important to them—how they can achieve their goals.

\*

"Speak as common people do, but think as wise men do."—Aristotle

\*

Tell donors what projects and services their past gifts have supported.....how their gifts have changed and saved lives.

\*

Tell donors how uniquely positioned your organization is to make the community and world a better place.

\*

\*

Know where you are, where
you are going and what you
want to accomplish every
minute of a donor visit.

\*

\*

Identify with a donor's needs and problems during visits. Then give the donor a vision for how those needs and problems can be addressed.

\*

Talk in terms of the donor's interests, what they care about. If you have taken an interest in a donor, she/he will take an interest in you.

\*

\*

Don't jump ahead in the conversational layering process with a donor. Slow down and first secure the donor's interest, time and attention.

\*

Match the donor's tempo and rhythm of speech. It will give the impression that you are like the donor, which will put her/him at ease.

\*

Share with donors why you have passion for your organization.

\*

*

Paint a picture with your words.

*

Always encourage a donor to understand the importance of taking action.

*

Know your organization's funding priorities. Be able to explain your organization's pressing needs to a donor.

*

\*

Communicate through images….the glistening, new building….the smiling, happy students. Use words that will inspire.

\*

\*

Agreement is an emotional bond that can bring you and the donor together.

\*

Remember during your visits......donors give for their own reasons, not yours.

\*

Every word counts in a successful donor visit

\*

\*

Use the donor's name during a visit. People are proud of their names and it makes them feel important.

\*

Remember......Big gifts come from the heart.

\*

\*

Eliminate 'fillers and sounds' from your speech….say bye-bye to "uh", "um", "you see", "you know", sighs, chuckling and throat clearing.

\*

The greater sense of urgency you can create with a donor, the more likely they will act on your request for money or your call for action.

\*

\*

There are four areas where you can focus your communication: Organization, campaign, self or donor. If you focus on the first three, your donor is outnumbered 3 to 1.

\*

\*

Donors remember vivid stories, not your exact words. Build an emotional connection by using stories about other donors and to make your points

\*

Humor builds rapport. Laughter is a form of approval. Use yourself as an example or victim of a joke....it is safe humor and it works.

\*

Try taking written notes during a donor visit. It shows the donor that their words are valuable.

\*

\*

If you have a habit of an upward inflection at the end of your sentences, lose it. This is an annoying habit.

\*

Find shared experiences or commonalities with a donor. Connect with food, sports, travel, family, fashion, wine, etc. Finding agreement is an emotional bond.

\*

Use a pause between important statements. Donors will view you as intelligent, confident, and analytical.

\*

\*

When expressing interest
in what a donor is saying,
soften your voice and your
smile.

\*

# May I Ask You a Few Questions?

Questions are the heart of the relationship and giving process….the engagement process.

*

Donors appreciate being asked important questions.

*

Fundraising is about what you ask, not what you say.

*

Ask questions that donors want to respond to.

*

Asking donors the right questions at the right times will lead to information and agreement.

*

\*

# The most productive and important sentence in any fundraiser's presentation always ends with a question.

\*

\*

Donors only reveal 25% of what is on their minds. It is your job to get the other 75% by asking questions and gently probing.

\*

Learn and practice asking donors questions. Questions gather information, establish your credibility and uncover needs.

\*

By demonstrating that you know how to ask intelligent and relevant questions, you demonstrate higher levels of credibility, competence and value.

\*

\*

Asking strategic questions sets you apart from the competition. It enriches and deepens your conversations.

\*

The person asking questions is in control of the visit.

\*

\*

Earn the right to ask questions. Ask "May I ask you a few questions?" A "Yes" response gives you an instant connection and the right to proceed.

\*

\*

Donors are reluctant to open up until you have established credibility. You must earn the right to probe into the donor's thoughts, feelings and concerns. To establish and build credibility, ask a series of short answer, easy to ask and answer questions such as....

- "How many...."
- "Is your...."
- "Do you....."
- "When was...."
- "Would you...."

\*

Asking questions shows interest. If you have taken an interest in a donor, the donor will take an interest in you.

\*

Donors do not always understand their needs and how to satisfy them. Through questioning, you help the donor in this discovery process.

\*

Find out what the donor wants and give it to her/him.

\*

Manage the scope of your questions. Begin with narrowly defined questions and then broaden the scope to gather opinions and values.

\*

Question to uncover needs. Your organization, project or campaign can then fill those needs.

\*

Ask questions about giving….what organizations does the donor support, why do they support those organizations and how much do they give.

\*

*

Asking donors strategic questions is the most important skill you should learn. It allows you to engage more donors in more productive conversations.

*

*

Ask questions about the donor's past, their experiences, likes, dislikes, vacations, colleges. Donors are proud of what they have done.

*

After you ask a question, be silent.

*

Ask questions in which donors would have to agree. Get the donor saying "Yes".

*

\*

Don't ask mindless questions. Every question you ask should add value in the engagement process by uncovering information or clarifying a point.

\*

\*

Acknowledge the donor's comments by saying "I understand" and "I appreciate" and gently probe with questions. Repeat this process over and over. Make this your pattern of communication.

\*

\*

Ask questions about money......the donor's views, thoughts, ideas.

\*

When questioning a donor, be a caring counselor instead of a prosecuting attorney.

\*

Once a donor acknowledges an issue as important, gently probe deeper to understand why it is important:
- "To what extent...."
- "What about...."
- "Have you ever...."
- "How does...."
- "What would happen...."

\*

\*

Use open door questions and explore topics with the donor:
- "How do you feel about...."
- "What do you think about...."
- "How do you see....."

\*

Use "Why" questions to discover the roots of a problem. Use "How" questions to uncover ways to improve.

\*

Tell me more questions:
- "And then what...."
- "How do you mean....."
- "Like what?"
- "What else?"

\*

\*

Power questions gather information:
- "What do you like about…."
- "Why….."
- "What has been your experience….."
- "What have you found….."

\*

How to respond to donor answers: Acknowledge, and then clarify by asking 1 or 2 information gathering questions.

\*

Even if you have met with a donor many times, ask a few probing questions to make sure you are up-to-date on new developments.

\*

\*

When you are asked
a question by a donor,
sometimes respond with
"How do you mean?" to
understand the donor's
perspective.

\*

*

Give donors an opportunity to say "Yes" or "No." Add, "Or No" at the end of any positive statement. It's a great way to let donors know that you are more interested in dealing with their needs, rather than pursuing your interests or those of your organization.

*

*

Be humble. Show the donor you do not know everything. Ask for help through a question. Donors are happy to help.

*

It is better to ask the right questions, strategic questions, instead of random question after random question.

*

Questions allow you to offer ideas and discuss decisions.

*

\*

If you understand how to make a donor curious with questions, you will always be successful.

\*

What makes donors curious and wanting more information? Glimpses of value....newness.... exclusivity....partial information. Curiosity is a good trait of happy people.

\*

Asking strategic questions allows you to engage more donors in more productive conversations.

\*

\*

Deep thinking questions:
- "What gives you joy?"
- "What are your strengths?"
- "What do you dream about?"
- "What do you cry about?"

\*

Make a list of 20 great questions........the most engaging and powerful questions you can create and then use them.

\*

Question your way to a gift.

\*

# Learn to Listen

Listen to donors. It is one of the highest compliments you can pay someone.

*

75/25 Principle of Engagement with donors.....75% - Listening......25% - Questions and Talking

*

Learn to listen. Pause before speaking, for additional comments from the donor. Silence draws donors out.

*

*

Listen with your heart and your eyes. Look and feel the emotion. Truly understand the meaning of what the donor is saying.

*

\*

Sometimes you have to be silent to be heard.

\*

The more you say, the less the donor remembers.

\*

One way to improve your listening skills is to spend more time listening.

\*

Listen....you are preparing the donor to listen to you.

\*

\*

Donors love to talk about themselves. They want to talk about their issues, problems and concerns. Listen, listen, listen.

\*

\*

# It is impossible to listen too much.

\*

*

Most of the things that can go wrong in a donor visit happen when your mouth is open.

*

Focus on what the donor is saying.....not what she/he may say next or what you may say next.

*

Add a few nods when listening.....they suggest that you are really listening and interested in what the donor is saying.

*

Listen for importance, the weight a donor assigns to your organization, project, campaign, benefits, time frame and cost.

\*

Listen to the donor's perceived needs. These are easier to fulfill than creating your own.

\*

Listen between the lines.

\*

Once donors feel genuinely heard, they will give and trust you with more information.

\*

Talking is sharing. Listening is caring.

\*

# The Power of Nonverbal Signals

Did you know that 55% of the information expressed during a donor visit is nonverbal communication? When measured against words at 7% and tone of voice at 38%, you can see the huge impact of nonverbal communication.

*

Nonverbal communication is how attitudes and feelings are communicated.

*

Smile. It says I like you, I am happy to be with you.

*

\*

Are your donor's nonverbal cues in alignment with their words? The message is from the heart when nonverbal and verbal communication is aligned.

\*

Do a body check during a donor visit to make sure your words are matched with your nonverbal gestures and signals.

\*

\*

Donors cannot hide what they are feeling. Nonverbal signals will present themselves reflecting the donor's true feelings.

\*

*

Make a positive, nonverbal first impression. Dress properly, stand tall and have a friendly handshake.

*

Smile from your heart. A true genuine smile is worth a million words.

*

Sit in an active, positive position and face the donor. Lean forward, have your feet flat on the ground, your legs should not be crossed. Make good eye contact and use open hand gestures.

*

\*

Look at these areas for nonverbal signals:
- Face
- Body Angle
- Arms
- Legs
- Hands

\*

Do not violate the donor's intimate space, which is up to 18 inches away from you.

\*

Scan signals and decide what types of signals the donor is sending and plan your response.

\*

Mention nonverbal cues you observe in the home or business.....a trophy, a picture, a photo.

\*

Your goal is to manage both the donor's nonverbal signals and your own…. to respond accurately and quickly to signals.

\*

\*

# A single gesture has little meaning. Look for groupings of nonverbal signals and their consistency.

\*

\*

Be aware of all the donor's nonverbal signals and their meaning:
- Yes Signals – Open and receptive
- Caution Signals – Obstacles, go slowly
- No Signals – Stop and re-direct

\*

Be aware of your own nonverbal signals. How does the donor perceive your signals? Are they a match for your verbal messages?

\*

When you observe these signals, you have Yes Signals:
- Face – Smiling, friendly
- Body Angle – Leaning toward you
- Arms – Open, relaxed
- Legs – Toward you, not crossed
- Hands – Open, relaxed

\*

When you observe these signals, you have Caution Signals:
- Face – Tense, doubt
- Body Angle – Leaning away from you
- Arms – Tense, crossed
- Legs – Crossed
- Hands – Fidgeting with objects, clasped

\*

When you observe these signals, you have No Signals:
- Face – Angry, tense
- Body Angle – Leaning far away from you
- Arms – Tightly crossed
- Legs – Crossed, away from you
- Hands – Fists, tucked into arms

\*

*

Respond to all signals from the donor with Yes Signals. Draw out the donor's true feelings when you observe clusters of Caution and No Signals by asking open-ended questions:
- "What are your...."
- "What do you think...."
- "Would you...."

*

A key is to not let Caution Signals become No Signals. Express understanding and change your approach to the donor.

*

Ask questions for clarification if you are ever confused about a donor's nonverbal signals and how you are reading them.

*

\*

# Never ask a donor for money unless you have Yes Signals.

\*

# Ask for the Action

Asking for money or the next action from the donor, is less like a dramatic, emotion filled moment and more like a joint conclusion that you and the donor arrive at together.

*

Know what you want and ask the donor for it.

*

Giving money is basically an emotional response and decision.

*

\*

Reflect the donor's own language into your action or solution—the one that takes you to a deeper level with the donor and solves their need or problem.

\*

\*

Use the knowledge you have gained by asking questions and listening to tailor how and what you ask a donor.

\*

*

Generously use the word "you" when summarizing what you heard. Personalize the ask for the action based on your questioning and listening.

*

When asking for money, ask for a specific amount for a specific purpose. Tell the donor how the money will benefit others.

*

Match the benefits of giving with the donors needs. Recognize the donor's needs and give your project, campaign or organization as the solution.

*

\*

Create a sense of urgency. The project must be funded <u>now</u> to save and change lives. Make an emotional connection to <u>now</u>....why the gift is needed <u>now</u>.

\*

When asking for the action, use "we" not "I" in the ask and statements related to the ask.

\*

Emphasize how uniquely positioned your organization is to change and save lives.

\*

Make it clear to the donor that their gift will be the cornerstone and key to the success of the project or campaign.

\*

Use check or feedback questions when summarizing and confirming what you have heard from the donor:

- "How does that sound?"
- "How would that work?"
- "What do you think?"

\*

When asking for money or the next action, get agreement and be specific...."Would you consider joining others and......."

\*

Incorporate the donor's needs and issues into your ask, your solution. Make it clear that you have heard the donor and you "get it".

\*

\*

# Be completely silent after any ask. Wait as long as it takes for a response.

\*

# Opportunity Knocks, in Objections

After your ask for the action, any question posed by the donor should be considered a positive sign. Objections indicate interest and the need for clarification.

*

Stay committed to your ask, and if it was for money, your gift.

*

Understand that objections are true issues that must be resolved before moving forward.

*

Ask the donor if there are any concerns....give the donor verbal approval to have an objection.

\*

# You cannot resolve a vague objection.

\*

\*

Objections connect you to the real thinking of a donor.
- Acknowledge the concern
- Ask a question to narrow down the objection

\*

Identify each individual objection. Address each issue, one at a time. Each objection must be resolved before you move on to the next one.

\*

Probe an objection to understand. Ask open-ended questions.
- "I can understand that. What do we have to do to resolve this issue so we can move ahead?"
- "I know it is a concern. May I ask why it is a concern?"

\*

\*

Use the donor's exact language when you respond to a specific concern.

\*

Use a donor success story to illustrate a point.

\*

The suppose test:
- "Suppose you felt….."
- "Suppose that condition did not exist….."
- "Suppose that was not a consideration….."

\*

Whenever you get stuck, acknowledge what the donor has said and gently probe. By acknowledging and probing you are demonstrating that you have listened and heard the donor.

\*

The donor says "Yes" to your money request. Cement the gift.

- "Your generous gift will help change and save lives. You made the right choice. Congratulations!"

\*

# Create a Lasting Impression

At the conclusion of your visit, thank the donor and refer to something personal you learned during the visit:
- "Enjoy the ballgame tomorrow night."
- "Have fun with your grandkids next weekend."
- "Good luck with your swimming workouts."

\*

There is one last comment for you to make. Touch the donor's heart with a comment and a question about a personal item found near their front door. You will leave the donor glowing and talking about something heartfelt:
- "That is a beautiful painting. Who is the artist?"
- "What a wonderful family photograph. Where was it taken?"
- "Your plants look so healthy. Do you enjoy gardening?"
- .....and Thank You for inviting me into your lovely home. I truly enjoyed our visit."

\*

May all your donor visits be successful visits.

Printed in the United States
By Bookmasters